P9-CDB-279

Discarded by MVCL

Gabby Douglas

By Jon M. Fishman

AMAZING ATHLETES

⌐ **Lerner Publications Company • Minneapolis**

MOUNT VERNON CITY LIBRARY
315 SNOQUALMIE
MOUNT VERNON, WA 98273

Copyright © 2013 by Lerner Publishing Group, Inc.

All rights reserved. International copyright secured. No part of this book may be reproduced, stored in a retrieval system, or transmitted in any form or by any means—electronic, mechanical, photocopying, recording, or otherwise—without the prior written permission of Lerner Publishing Group, Inc., except for the inclusion of brief quotations in an acknowledged review.

Lerner Publications Company
A division of Lerner Publishing Group, Inc.
241 First Avenue North
Minneapolis, MN 55401 U.S.A.

Website address: www.lernerbooks.com

Library of Congress Cataloging-in-Publication Data available.
ISBN 978-1-4677-1311-5

Manufactured in the United States of America
1 – MG – 12/31/12

TABLE OF CONTENTS

Gabby performs at the 2012 Olympic Games in London, England.

LONDON CALLING

Gabby Douglas stood at the end of the runway. Her pink **leotard** twinkled under the lights. She was competing in the women's gymnastics individual **all-around** final at the 2012 Olympic Games in London, England. Thousands of fans in the stadium cheered for Gabby. Millions more watched on television.

The all-around at the Olympics is the world's biggest gymnastics competition. Gymnasts from all over the world came to London to try to take home the gold medal. Gabby wanted it for herself.

The first event in the all-around was the **vault**. Gabby raced down the runway. She jumped from the **vaulting horse** and flew high into the air. She spun and twisted before landing on her feet. It was a great vault! Gabby's **score** put her in first place.

Gabby twists off the vaulting horse during the all-around competition.

London 2012

Gabby keeps her eyes on the bar.

Next was the **uneven bars**. This is usually Gabby's best event. She soars higher above the bars than other gymnasts. She flies from bar to bar with ease. Gabby put up a good score. But she finished third behind Russia's Aliya Mustafina and Victoria Komova.

Gabby would have to do better in the final two events if she wanted to win the all-around. But she wasn't worried. "My message is to never quit, never give up," Gabby said. "When you have a little trouble here and there, just keep fighting. In the end, it will pay off."

The **balance beam** was up next. This event had given Gabby trouble in the past. At the 2012 Visa Championships in Saint Louis, Missouri, she fell off the beam. If she had not fallen, Gabby would have won the USA national championship. She needed to do better in London if she wanted the gold medal.

Gabby's nickname is the Flying Squirrel. She soars so high, it almost looks like she's flying.

This time, Gabby stayed on the beam. The crowd cheered as she pulled off a series of **back handsprings**. After landing a good **dismount**, Gabby broke into a huge smile. She knew that she had done enough to win the event.

Gabby pulls off a great performance on the balance beam.

Russian gymnast Victoria Komova performs during the all-around.

Gabby's score on the balance beam was the best of the day. But Victoria Komova was close behind. With only one event to go, Gabby had a slim overall lead on Komova. If Gabby could put up a good score on the **floor exercise**, she would win the gold medal!

Gabby lived on this street in Virginia Beach, Virginia, when she was very young.

"A WINNER'S SPIRIT"

Gabrielle Christina Victoria Douglas was born on December 31, 1995, in Virginia Beach, Virginia. Gabby has two older sisters named Arielle and Joyelle. She has an older brother named John. Gabby's mother, Natalie Hawkins, raised the family. Timothy Douglas, Gabby's father, left the family when Gabby was a young child.

Arielle saw her younger sister's talent for gymnastics when Gabby was just four years old. "I'd put her on the floor and she'd be doing splits," said Arielle. "She was just super flexible from day one." Arielle taught Gabby to do cartwheels. Then Gabby taught herself to do cartwheels one-handed.

Gabby loved gymnastics. She practiced at home. "I was just flipping around and hitting tables and breaking stuff," Gabby said. It soon became clear that she needed proper lessons.

Arielle thought Gabby should get gymnastics training. But Natalie didn't think it was a good idea. She was afraid Gabby would get hurt. Finally, Natalie agreed. Gabby began lessons.

This is the gymnastics center where Gabby trained in Virginia Beach.

It was clear that Gabby had a bright future in gymnastics. She had the talent. And she was ready to work hard to make herself better. One day when Gabby was just seven years old, she came home from the gym with a fever. "She went to bed, slept it off and woke up and got back in the gym the next day," said Gabby's mother. "That's when we knew she had a winner's attitude, a winner's spirit."

In 2006, Gabby went to a gymnastics camp at the Karolyi Ranch near Houston, Texas. The camp is run by Bela and Martha Karolyi. The

Karolyis are famous gymnastics coaches. They could see Gabby's talent. They knew she had a chance to compete in the Olympics someday if she worked hard enough and got the right coaching.

Gabby told her mother that she wanted to work with gymnastics coach Liang Chow. Coach Chow had trained Shawn Johnson for the 2008 Olympic Games. Johnson won the silver medal in the all-around competition.

Coach Chow and Shawn Johnson celebrate after Shawn Johnson won the gold medal on the balance beam at the 2008 Olympics.

Gabby practices gymnastics six days a week. She often has two practices in one day.

There was only one problem. Coach Chow lived in West Des Moines, Iowa. Gabby would have to move if she wanted to work with Chow. In 2010, Gabby's mother finally agreed to send her daughter to Iowa. "I must have lost my marbles," Natalie said. "But she wanted this more than anything."

Gabby moved near Des Moines, Iowa, to train with Liang Chow.

TO IOWA AND BEYOND

Moving from Virginia to Iowa was hard for fourteen-year-old Gabby. At first, she "cried and cried." She missed her family. And her family missed Gabby. "Letting her go wasn't easy," Natalie said.

Gabby lived with Travis and Missy Parton in Iowa. They welcomed Gabby into their lives.

Gabby began to work with Coach Chow and Shawn Johnson. She knew Gabby would have to work hard to reach her Olympic dreams. Johnson called Gabby "a ball of raw talent" when they first met.

Johnson and Coach Chow quickly helped

Gabby poses with her biggest fans: her mother *(front, second from right)*, her sisters Arielle *(front, second from left)* and Joyelle *(behind Arielle)*, her brother, John *(behind their mom)*, and Travis and Missy Parton *(right)*.

Gabby mold her raw talent into world-class gymnastics performances. Gabby's first big national **meet** was the 2010 CoverGirl Classic in Chicago, Illinois. She finished with the third-best score on the balance beam and the sixth-best on the vault. Later that year, Gabby competed in the U.S. Junior National Championships in Hartford, Connecticut. She finished fourth in the all-around competition.

Gabby had left junior competitions behind by 2011. She was ready to face the best gymnasts of any age. In August, Gabby competed at the Visa Championships. This is the national championship meet for USA Gymnastics. She finished third on the uneven bars and took home a bronze medal.

Gabby likes all kinds of music. Two of her favorite artists are Katy Perry and Drake.

Gabby took part in the biggest competition of her young career in November. She traveled with her USA Gymnastics teammates to Tokyo, Japan, to compete in the 2011 World Gymnastics Championships. At 15 years of age, Gabby was the youngest gymnast at the meet. She put up the fifth-best score on the uneven bars. She also helped her team take first place in the team all-around event.

Gabby flies around the uneven bars at the 2011 World Championships.

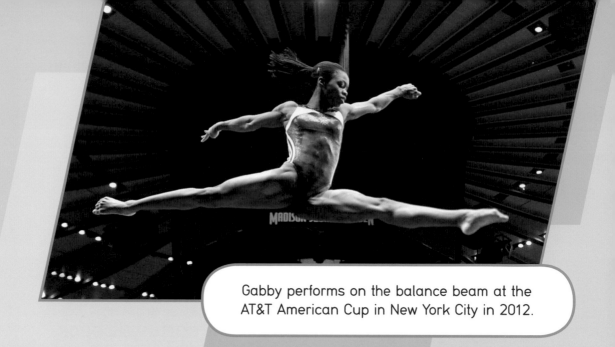

Gabby performs on the balance beam at the AT&T American Cup in New York City in 2012.

MAKING THE TEAM

Gabby became known as one of the best young gymnasts in the country. Moving to Iowa to work with Coach Chow had paid off. She was ready for big things in 2012.

Gabby competed at the AT&T American Cup held at Madison Square Garden in New York City. She shined in all four events and finished with the highest all-around score of the day.

But Gabby was competing as an **alternate**. Her scores didn't count. Still, she showed that she was at the top of her game.

Gabby was no longer an alternate by the time the 2012 Visa Championships arrived in June. This was the last big competition before the **Olympic trials**. Gabby tried a series of back handsprings on the balance beam for her first event. But she lost her footing and leaned out and away from the beam as the crowd gasped. She slipped off the beam and onto the floor.

Gabby was upset to start the competition with a fall. But she quickly put the beam out of her mind. She put up good scores on the vault and floor events. The final event was the uneven

Gabby always wears lip gloss, even in the gym. She carries some with her wherever she goes.

bars. Gabby spun and flew around the bars as only she can. Then she landed a good dismount. Gabby broke out in a huge smile and pumped her fist to the crowd. Her score on the uneven bars was the best of the day. Gabby finished the meet just barely behind Jordyn Wieber for second place.

Gabby gets a hug from Coach Chow during the 2012 Visa Championships.

The nation's best gymnasts met in San Jose, California, in July for the Olympic trials. Gabby was ready for anything. The meet ended with Gabby and Wieber scoring the most points. But this time, Gabby came out on top. She was going to the Olympic Games in London!

"All of this hard work has definitely paid off," Gabby said. "I just can't wait to wear those red, white, and blue stripes down my back. It felt like a dream come true."

Gabby celebrates a great performance at the Olympic trials.

Tower Bridge in London, England, is decorated with the Olympic rings.

GOLDEN GABBY

The Olympic Games is the biggest sporting event in the world. Millions of people tune in on television. Olympic medal winners go down in history as the finest athletes of their time. All eyes would be on Gabby and her teammates for the women's gymnastics **qualifying round**.

Team USA put up good scores and finished first in the qualifying round. They advanced to the team all-around final. The top two gymnasts from each country in the qualifying round advance to the individual all-around final. Aly Raisman had Team USA's best scores. Gabby finished second.

Aly Raisman *(left)* and Gabby react to qualifying for the individual all-around.

Team USA took the lead on the first event and never looked back. They had the highest scores on three of the four events to win the gold medal! "We knew we could do it," Raisman said. "We just had to pull out all the stops."

If you unscramble Gabby Douglas's last name, you get "USA gold."

Team USA receives their gold medals. *From left:* Jordyn Wieber, Gabby, McKayla Maroney, Aly Raisman, and Kyla Ross.

Next was the individual all-around. Gabby was in first place after three events. She had a slim lead on Victoria Komova. Gabby's family and millions of fans hung on every move. Gabby's final event was the floor exercise. She danced and flipped around the mat. She grinned at the judges as the crowd clapped along to the music. "I love this routine," she said. "I can express myself."

Gabby competes on the floor exercise for the individual all-around gold medal.

Gabby's floor exercise score of 15.033 was the fourth-best of the day. She hopped up and down and waved to the crowd. Komova could not catch up. Gabby had won the individual all-around gold medal! She hugged Coach Chow as the crowd chanted, "Go Gabby!"

Gabby had come a long way since moving to Iowa by herself to train with Coach Chow. Her mother knew that all the hard work and time apart was worth it. "You have to take those chances," Natalie said. "If it works out, great, if not, have no regrets."

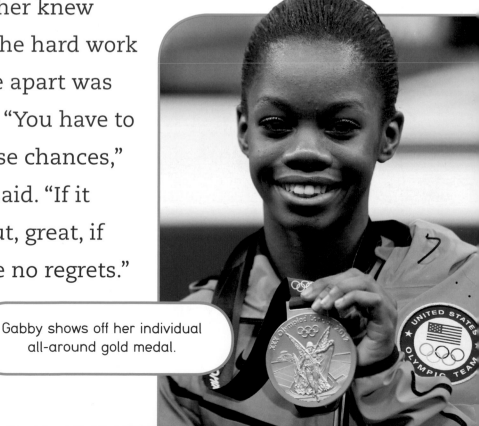

Gabby shows off her individual all-around gold medal.

Gabby gets a high five from First Lady Michelle Obama on *The Tonight Show with Jay Leno.*

Gabby stayed busy as an Olympic gold medalist. She appeared on *The Tonight Show with Jay Leno* with First Lady Michelle Obama. Her face is on products such as Kellogg's Corn Flakes cereal boxes. And Gabby plans to compete at the 2016 Olympic Games in Rio de Janeiro, Brazil. But for now, Gabby will enjoy memories of her time in London. "It was just a dream come true," she said. "I wanted to dance and I wanted to cry at the same time. I was just so happy."

Selected Career Highlights

2012   Won individual all-around gold medal
at Olympic Games
Helped Team USA win
team all-around gold
medal at Olympic Games
Finished second in
individual all-around at Visa
Championships
Finished with highest score in individual all-around competing as an
alternate at the AT&T American Cup

2011   Helped Team USA finish first at World Gymnastics Championships
Finished third in uneven bars at Visa Championships

2010   Finished fourth in individual all-around at U.S. Junior National
Championships
Competed in first national meet at the CoverGirl Classic
Moved to West Des Moines, Iowa, to train with Liang Chow

2004   Won the individual all-around competition for her age level at
Virginia State Championships

2002   Began formal gymnastics training

Glossary

all-around: an individual event in the women's competition in which athletes compete in the vault, uneven bars, balance beam, and floor exercise

alternate: in gymnastics, a person who competes as a possible replacement for another gymnast. An alternate's scores only count if another gymnast is unable to finish the competition.

back handspring: a jump backward onto the hands, followed by quick jumps to the feet

balance beam: an event during which the gymnast performs on a long, narrow bar. A balance beam is 4 inches wide and 16 feet long.

dismount: the act of jumping off the uneven bars or balance beam to end a routine

floor exercise: in women's gymnastics, an event in which the gymnast performs dance steps and tumbling moves to music on a 40-square-foot mat

leotard: a tight uniform worn by gymnasts

meet: an event at which a number of gymnastics contests are held

Olympic trials: a competition to decide which gymnasts will compete in the Olympic Games

qualifying round: in gymnastics, the first competition of a meet. In the Olympics, the top eight teams in the qualifying round advance to the team final round.

score: in gymnastics, the number of points awarded for an athlete's performance. A group of judges gives a score for a routine. Good routines receive higher scores. The gymnast loses points each time a mistake is made.

uneven bars: an event in which the gymnast performs on a set of 8-foot-long bars. One bar is set 8 feet high. The second bar is set about 5.5 feet high.

vault: in gymnastics, an event in which the gymnast runs down a runway, jumps onto a springboard, pushes with the hands off the vaulting horse, and lands on a mat

vaulting horse: a piece of gymnastics equipment with a padded body used in the vault event

Further Reading & Websites

Olsen, Leigh. *Going for Gold: The 2008 U.S. Gymnastics Team*. New York: Price Stern Sloan, 2008.

Savage, Jeff. *Carly Patterson*. Minneapolis: Lerner Publications Company, 2005.

Savage, Jeff. *Top 25 Gymnastics Skills, Tips, and Tricks*. Berkeley Heights, NJ: Enslow Publishers, 2011.

Gabrielle Douglas: 2012 Olympic Gold Medalist & AA Champion
http://www.gabrielledouglas.com
Gabby's official website features photos, videos, and information about Gabby and the sport of gymnastics.

Sports Illustrated Kids
http://www.sikids.com
The *Sports Illustrated Kids* website covers all sports, including gymnastics.

USA Gymnastics
http://www.usagym.org
The official site of USA Gymnastics has biographies of athletes, information about competitions, and much more.

Index

Photo Acknowledgments

The images in this book are used with the permission of: © John Todd/ISI/CORBIS, p. 4; © David Eulitt/Kansas City Star/MCT via Getty Images, pp. 5, 6, 29; Cheng Min/Xinhua/Sipa USA/Newscom, p. 8; © Streeter Lecka/Getty Images, pp. 9, 27; © Splash News/CORBIS, pp. 10, 12; © Amy Sancetta/AP/CORBIS, p. 13; © J. Mrachina (www.flickr.com/w4nd3rl0st)/Getty Images, p. 15; © Scott Halleran/Getty Images for Kelloggs, p. 16; © Adam Pretty/Getty Images, p. 18; © Timothy A. Clary/AFP/Getty Images, p. 19; © Jeff Roberson/AP/CORBIS, p. 21; © Jae C. Hong/AP/CORBIS, p. 22; © Johannes Eisele/AFP/Getty Images, p. 23; © Gregory Bull/CORBIS, p. 24; © Ben Stansall/AFP/Getty Images, p. 25; © Chang W. Lee/The New York Times/Redux, p. 26; © Margaret Norton/NBC/NBCU Photo Bank via Getty Images, p. 28.

Front cover: Mohammad Khursheed/Cal Sport Media/Newscom.

Main body text set in Caecilia LT Std 55 Roman 16/28.
Typeface provided by Adobe Systems.

MOUNT VERNON CITY LIBRARY